Statman's Racing "Bibles"- Using Statistics To Increase Your Chance Of Backing A Winner

BOOK THREE – ALL-WEATHER RACING BOTH UK AND IRELAND

Sea Trivass AKA "The Statman"

Introduction.

Do you want to increase your chances of finding the winners or equally importantly, which horse who may best left alone of an afternoon or evening? That was my concept when I wrote my UK NH Statman book and my Irish NH Statman book (also available on Amazon), to help everyone to narrow down the contenders, and nothing has changed with this version, which only covers All-Weather racing for both the United Kingdom and Ireland.

This is not a book for the faint-hearted – it is a long-list of statistics by track and covers most sensible options to help you decide whether to have a bet – or not – but by now I would guess you are itching for examples?

So, if you already know…

- Which two trainers have a combined strike rate of just 9.23% in non-handicaps at Chelmsford – but a profit of £851.24 to £1 stakes, a return on investment of over 1300%

- Which jockey has a ridiculous 60% strike rate at Dundalk in non-handicaps

- Which racecourse would see you in clover to the tune of £303.86 to £1 stakes if you simply backed horses who won last time out in handicaps

- Which trainer has a strike rate of 33.33% in Kempton handicaps and a return on investment of over 100%

- Which sire has a 15.19% strike rate in non-handicaps at Lingfield and shows a profit of close to £500 from just the 79 qualifiers

…then you really don't need this book - though I suspect the majority will be pleasantly surprised by those disclosures (and the hundreds others included below) see this for what it is – a way to help you to decide when and where to bet on All-Weather racing with all the figures above and literally hundreds more (good and bad) below.

A Little About Your Author.

No-one wants to read about me, and I don't need to tell you my life story either, but a little background may at least let you know where I come from, what I know – and why the following pages may well prove well worth reading if you want to increase your chances of making a profit from the horses.

I have been involved in the sport for over 40 years now, starting on the local paper with a weekly article where I was paid the grand sum of a fiver, in the days when I had to write in block capitals with a pen and paper – and cycle to the offices to stick it through their letterbox every Sunday – and no, those weren't the good old days!

Since then I have been to college where I got a Distinction in Quantitative Studies (or Stats to you and I), and for the last 20 years or so I have been a full-time freelance racing journalist writing for all sorts – including The Independent, BetDaq, Alan Brazil Racing Club, What Really Wins, Australian Thoroughbred News, The Daily Sport, Press Association, Post Racing, Worldofsport, Timeform, and numerous others in a rich and varied career.

Like most (all?) punters, I have spent my lifetime searching for the Holy Grail – the system or the tipster who provides you with winner after winner, with all the associated dreams of wealth and happiness, but I have finally drawn the same conclusion that you should – it simply does not exist. If you are reading this thinking "Eureka" turn away now – the stats I have put together will not make you rich overnight – in fact they will undoubtedly find more losers than winners – but what they will do is narrow down the field to the likelier winners on any given racing day, if we assume past history can and does repeat itself – something nobody can ever guarantee.

What I can tell you is that this is my living – and if you stick rigidly to the rules suggested here and bet accordingly, putting in the necessary work to go with it – you won't go far wrong IN THE LONG TERM – overnight success belongs in fairy tales I am sorry to say.

Other books will follow so please look out for future publications with the plans so far including Cheltenham Profiling, UKs Flat (turf), Irish Flat turf, Aintree profiling, Royal Ascot profiling, and glorious Goodwood profiling plus "Who's The Daddy" when I will look at sires and how to make the most of their progeny. UK National Hunt Racing and Irish National Hunt Racing have already been published and are available on Amazon.

Index

What is this all about?

"Lies, damned lies, and statistics" is a much-used quote attributed to Mark Twain, and the truth is, anyone good with figures can make the statistics tell whatever story they want them to tell – but that is not my remit, you will be delighted to know. In my years working as the anonymous "Statman" I produced a monthly racing/betting article looking to find profitable ways to bet on horse racing in the United Kingdom and Ireland with great success – but I was never stupid enough to put them all down in one place and lose the gig – stupid, maybe, but that stupid – no.

When the publication (or my part of it) came to an end, someone suggested to me I produce a compendium – but that would have included a lot of out-of-date information and would be potentially conning the paying public, something I would never knowingly do. So, a new idea was born – how about a list of preferred statistics by racecourse, all accurate at the time of writing, and all easy to refer to on a daily basis.

For early clarity, race statistics are based over the last 20 years (1st January 2002 to the 20th December 2022 when I turned off the wifi to ensure no more updates) , sire, trainer and jockey statistics over the last 11 (1st January 2012 to the 20th December 2022) – the reason for this is simple enough, jockeys and trainers come and go as do the actual horses – but the results remain the same, so if the top weight is profitable to follow at Track A that could or even should continue – but there is no point in telling you that Willie Carson was profitable to follow at Course B when he is (sadly) long retired or that Busted was a top-sire when he passed away years ago.

How To Make The Most Of This book.

Let me start with one sad but very simple piece of news – you will almost always make more money backing at Betfair SP than you will with the starting price from the bookmakers – fact. For that reason, ALL my profits and losses are declared to Betfair SP and NOT bookmaker SP as we are looking to make money, end of, and I have taken into account the standard Betfair commission of 2% (correct at the time of writing) in all of my figures.

I have listed every National Hunt racecourse in Ireland in alphabetical order) – you simply go the course or courses you are interested in on any given day and look at the stats laid out for you.

Included at each course you will find the following information:

Backing To Win

Top Jockeys by strike rate

Top Jockeys by profit to £1 level stake at BSP (Betfair Starting Price)

Top Trainers by strike rate

Top Trainers by profit to £1 level stake BSP (Betfair Starting Price)

Most successful trainer jockey combos

Profit or loss by backing favourites

Profit or loss by backing second favourites

Profit or Loss by backing Top-Weights in handicaps

Top Five Profitable Sires to follow

Profit or Loss by backing last time out winners

And all listed by non-handicaps and handicaps.

Rules:

- All profits and losses are declared to BSP (Betfair Starting Price) to a nominal £1 stake and after an assumed deduction of 2% from all winning bets (Betfair commission at the time of writing).
- Figures declared for top-weights, favourites, and second favourites assume backing all horses if there were joint top weights, Co or Joint favourites and Co or Joint second favourites
- If any sector listed by profitability has less than five results in the black (profitable), only the profitable options will be listed.
- All figures have been based on sensible numbers – a minimum or 10 to qualify – the temptation was there to "interfere" but these are statistics (facts) so 10 will be the minimum for ALL categories come what may. A smaller number would not tell an accurate story, and a larger number would have seen numerous categories left completely unpopulated.
- I saw no point over-cluttering with empty sections. If there are less than five listed, there were less than five who qualified, or if the section is missing, there were no qualifiers.
- Do note - there is a new trend of "shared" training - for example horses that were trained by John Gosden are now trained by Thady and John Gosden – I cannot make allowances for this on historical data, so you need to look for yourselves as this appears to be an ever changing fact. Other examples would include William Muir and Chris Grassic, Charlie and Mark Johnston etc – I'm afraid you will have to spot those for yourself, but the yards remain the same, so if the stats say John Gosden – you can look for horses trained by Thady and John Gosden, and so on.
- You may note that I did NOT include "most winners" in any category – it was seriously considered, but it would be overloaded with trainers/jockeys who have been in the game the longest time with the biggest strings and thus not necessarily of any relevance.
- Bumpers have been deliberately ignored - there are simply not enough of them per track to make any data worthwhile or relevant.
- For those who think I dumped this directly from a database – I wish! Every line was painstakingly typed in by hand and although I can vouch for the accuracy of all the numbers, if there are any typos please forgive me, I am only human whatever others may tell you.

Gambling Harm

As I write the Gambling review is coming, and centre stage in many people's minds – but that is a discussion for elsewhere. This book is not meant to encourage anyone to gamble, and I urge you all to think twice before placing any bets to make sure you can afford your hobby. For me, racing is exciting and fun – it's not about the gambling, it's about pitting my wits against those who compile the odds – and trying to find a way to beat the bookmakers – I can do that with small **affordable** bets and suggest you do the same. Do NOT let gambling overcome you, do NOT bet more than you can afford to lose – and DO make the most of all the tools available with your bookmaker such as time outs and deposit limits if needed. Please please control your gambling (do not let it control you) and remember that help is available via the National Gambling Helpline (0808 8020 133), and online at Gamcare.org.uk with other services freely available.

How To Use This Book

I have listed all the UK and Irish courses in Alphabetical order, so on any given day:

1) Go to your publication of choice (I prefer the Racing Post www.racingpost.com) and look to see what meetings are on that day – you only need access to the free version you will be delighted to know.
2) Look for the course or courses mentioned and go to their pages
3) Refer to the statistics produced and look for any horses that "qualify"
4) Favourites – note the statistics are based on the Returned favourites – i.e., the horse or horses sent off favourite at the off and NOT the horses predicted favourite or at the head of the market some time before the off
5) Sires - you may need to look deeper or adjust your on-line settings to find the sires, but it isn't difficult to do
6) Jockeys and trainers are clearly annotated to the right of the horse's name
7) Top-weights in handicaps – look for the word handicap in the race title – the top-weight will be horse number one though remember to look at the weight the horse carries – if horse two three etc has/have the same weight (we ignore any jockey claims) they are joint-top-weights and should all be thought of accordingly.
8) Chases or Hurdles – the word chase (or steeplechase) will appear in the race title, or the word hurdle - simple as that
9) Dutching is an option I often employ when more than one horse qualifies for the same race. This involves splitting the bet according to the odds to achieve the same profit if any of them win. There are plenty available via your search engine of choice, but I use the one at oddschecker here https://www.oddschecker.com/betting-tools/dutching-calculator
10) Personally (and this is MY choice), I never consider a horse unless its trainer has an RTF figure (Running To Form) of at least 40% (preferably 50%) which is found on the Racing Post site beside the trainer's name- I don't care how good a horse is, if the stable are out of form it doesn't necessarily matter.
11) If there are more than 16 runners and the race is NOT a handicap bet in the "first four home" market on Betfair if punting each way.
12) Enjoy – and good luck on your journey to profit, using historical data as your guide.

So How Do I Find A Bet?

That my friend, is down to you! Have you ever seen the TV programme Ready Steady Cook? Contestants bring a bag of assorted unknown goodies, and the chefs then make a delicious meal from whatever they are given. This book is the bag of ingredients, and you are the chef! Some will try to use all the ingredients, others will want to leave some parts out, the choice is yours. By definition, if you find a highly profitable jockey at a particular track that may be a sorely tempting angle – but if you see a 5% strike rate then you know in advance that you may be waiting some time before he or she fires in the next winner with your money on it. That may be fine for some, while others will look for the best strike rates where the winners are more likely to flow – though with lower profit margins. Personally (and this is me, not you talking), I find a race I like the look of first, then head off to the statistics to see what comes out in the wash. I'll give you an example or two below of how I work – so wish me luck – but please note, these are statistics, they are facts from the past – I cannot guarantee they will repeat themselves, but they do imply a pattern for whatever reason, and have served me well enough over the years.

Examples.

I cannot make it clear enough to everyone that how you use these statistics is entirely up to you! Everyone will have their own preferred way to bet (or not to bet), some will be looking for one horse a week, some one a day – others may fancy a 10p Lucky 15 (four horses), the choice is entirely yours. Below is a way they can be used, it is not definitive, and nor is there a right and a wrong – it's your money you are risking after all.

When I look at a race (and that is MY view, not necessarily yours), I like to search for at least two positives in a race – plus the obligatory RTF figure of 40% or more (and personally I prefer 50%+). I am NOT looking for top of the list (quite often only one jockey or trainer will even be on the list for a particular race), but I am looking for a combination. As you can imagine when we have a total of 11 categories for any one race, whether that is over hurdles or over fences, giving examples that cover every option is impossible (if you covered 11 horses in trebles that would be 165 bets so hopefully you can see what I mean).

The only thing I have left to add is please don't take the numbers at face value. A profit of £23 is unimpressive at first glance – but if it came from only 10 qualifiers that figure is far more useful than if it came from 104 runners. I advise mentally dividing the number of runners by the profit figure – if the profit is bigger than the number of qualifiers we have over 100% return on investment each time, which makes it well worth a second look. Some will look for the best figures available for a race they plan to bet in regardless, others will look though all the races on any given day to see if anything fits – as they say, beauty is in the eye of the beholder, and this is yours to use as you see fit.

Example One – 7.00pm Kempton 7th January 2023

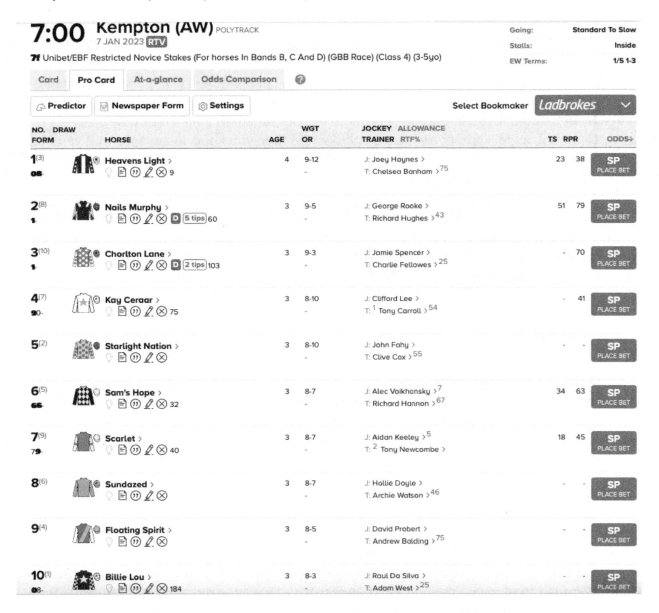

Please remember – the facts are here for YOU to use as you see fit – but this is how I would play the race.

Running down the lists for non-handicaps the notes I made were as follows:

No listed jockeys

Trainers Andrew Balding (+£208.58) and Clive Cox (+£125.27) are both in the top five for profit (and both have strike rates above 40%). Andrew Balding and David Probert head the profit list for trainer/jockey combos (+£220.66), giving them the edge, while my confidence in the horse as a selection is boosted by the stats telling me favourites and horses who won last time out are both showing losses, which is a black mark for the short-priced Nails Murphy. No qualifying sires (this can be toggled on and off via the settings by the way, it is switched off here so I can fit the race on a page!) This leaves me with two points for Floating Spirit (Andrew Balding) and one for Starlight Nation (Clive Cox) but with the first named trainer on a 75% RTF (as opposed to 55%), and a weakness in the market for the Cox horse (out to 22/1 at the off) I won't dutch on this occasion and would have a straight win bet

Result Floating Spirit Won 11/2, Starlight Nation a promising fourth at 22/1.

Example Two Southwell 7.00pm 10ᵗʰ January 2023

I shouldn't have – but I did!

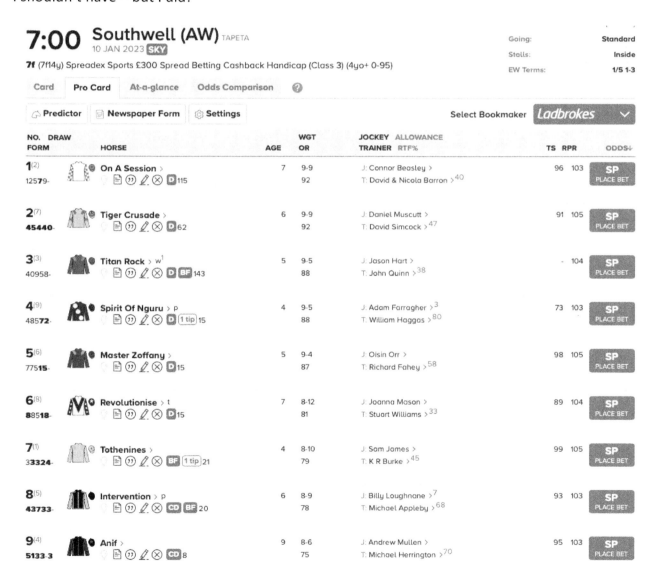

Ok so running through the stats for Southwell in brief and the following were noted:

No qualifying jockeys for this race
Two qualifying trainers - David Simcock (Tiger Crusade) with a strike rate of 32.35% and a profit of +£30.19 and Karl Burke (Tothenines) with a profit of £159.13 and a strike rate of 16.33%, with both trainers having an RTF figure of over 40% (my personal cut-off number). No other positive stats to go with BUT I also noted that top-weights have a big negative figure here, as do favourites and second favourites, and as both horses did not sit in any of those positions in a small field I dutched them both.

Result – Tiger Crusade won 10/1 (BSP 14.74) Tothenines fourth 9/1 (BSP 14.5) for a profit of 2.44 points on the bet – or £24.40 to a £10 stake

All-Weather Racecourses in alphabetical order:

Chelmsford City

Top jockeys by Strike Rate – non-handicaps

Name Of Jockey	Rides	Winners	Strike Rate	Profit/Loss to BSP
Frankie Dettori	33	13	39.39%	+£4.50
James Doyle	107	40	37.38%	+£11.44
Ryan Moore	82	27	32.93%	-£0.86
Jim Crowley	136	41	30.15%	+£72.73
Shane Gray	10	3	30.00%	+£19.13

Top jockeys by Strike Rate – handicaps

Name Of Jockey	Rides	Winners	Strike Rate	Profit/Loss to BSP
Ryan Moore	98	32	32.65%	+£42.51
Kevin Stott	68	21	30.88%	+£43.69
Frankie Dettori	26	7	26.92%	-£3.18
Sean Kirrane	20	5	25.00%	+£20.58
Connor Beasley	74	16	21.62%	+£42.81

Top jockeys by Profit – non-handicaps

Name Of Jockey	Rides	Winners	Strike Rate	Profit/Loss to BSP
Darragh Keenan	63	2	3.17%	+£434.13
Eoin Walsh	37	2	5.41%	+£387.05
Marc Monaghan	33	7	21.21%	+£135.92
Jimmy Quinn	46	2	4.35%	+£115.20
Rob Hornby	72	7	9.72%	+£110.95

Top jockeys by Profit – handicaps

Name Of Jockey	Rides	Winners	Strike Rate	Profit/Loss to BSP
Callum Shepherd	334	49	14.67%	+£247.93

Dougie Costello	215	23	10.70%	+£171.45
Christian Howarth	29	5	17.24%	+£146.14
George Wood	152	18	11.84%	+£120.03
Ben Curtis	151	21	13.91%	+£106.55

Top trainers by Strike Rate – non-handicaps

Name Of Trainer	Runners	Winners	Strike Rate	Profit/Loss to BSP
Ian Williams	19	7	36.84%	+£26.58
Saeed bin Suroor	130	41	31.54%	+£0.21
Roger Teal	10	3	30.00%	-£0.68
Charlie Appleby	106	30	28.30%	-£22.88
John Gosden	254	70	27.56%	-£11.02

Top trainers by Strike Rate – handicaps

Name Of Trainer	Runners	Winners	Strike Rate	Profit/Loss to BSP
Owen Burrows	30	9	30.00%	+£44.99
Sir Michael Stoute	93	24	25.81%	-£5.20
Simon Pearce	31	8	25.81%	+£71.37
John Gosden	99	23	23.23%	-£5.14
Saeed bin Suroor	140	32	22.86%	-£4.30

Top trainers by Profit – non-handicaps

Name Of Trainer	Runners	Winners	Strike Rate	Profit/Loss to BSP
Mohamed Moubarak	24	3	12.50%	+£462.82
John Butler	41	3	7.32%	+£388.42
Marco Botti	204	25	12.25%	+£158.65
Robyn Brisland	73	7	9.59%	+£141.49
Sir Mark Prescott Bt	139	13	9.35%	+£113.94

Top trainers by Profit – handicaps

Name Of Trainer	Runners	Winners	Strike Rate	Profit/Loss to BSP
Robert Cowell	226	26	11.50%	+£199.85
Henry Spiller	205	29	14.15%	+£191.20
Martin Bosley	48	3	6.25%	+£132.66
Mike Murphy and Michael Keady	17	1	5.88%	+£130.93
John Best and Karen Jewell	146	23	15.75%	+£128.62

Top trainer/jockey combos by Strike Rate – non-handicaps

Name of Trainer/Jockey	Qualifiers	Winners	Strike Rate	Profit/Loss to BSP
Saeed bin Suroor/Pat Cosgrave	15	9	60.00%	+£21.76
John Gosden/Frankie Dettori	20	10	50.00%	+£10.84
Charlie Appleby/James Doyle	15	7	46.67%	-£0.89
Hugo Palmer/James Doyle	18	8	44.44%	+£6.60
John Gosden/Jim Crowley	10	4	40.00%	+£6.17

Top trainer/jockey combos by Strike Rate – handicaps

Name of Trainer/Jockey	Qualifiers	Winners	Strike Rate	Profit/Loss to BSP
Sir Michael Stoute/Jim Crowley	10	6	60.00%	+£11.74
Stuart Williams/Jason Hart	12	6	50.00%	+£18.45
John Gosden/Frankie	13	6	46.15%	+£6.22

Dettori				
Simon Pearce/David Probert	11	5	45.45%	+£23.53
David Simcock/Martin Harley	14	6	42.86%	+£30.74

Top trainer/jockey combos by Profit – non-handicaps

Name of Trainer/Jockey	Qualifiers	Winners	Strike Rate	Profit/Loss to BSP
Sir Mark Prescott Bt/Luke Morris	86	8	9.30%	+£96.33
Ralph Beckett/Rob Hornby	16	5	31.25%	+£76.74
Mark Johnston/P J McDonald	28	5	17.86%	+£56.07
Jamie Osborne/Dougie Costello	17	5	29.41%	+£46.06
Archie Watson/Oisin Murphy	12	3	25.00%	+£37.55

Top trainer/jockey combos by Profit – handicaps

Name of Trainer/Jockey	Qualifiers	Winners	Strike Rate	Profit/Loss to BSP
Martin Bosley/George Wood	15	3	20.00%	+£165.66
Henry Spiller/Christian Howarth	20	5	25.00%	+£155.14
Michael Bell/Hayley Turner	10	3	30.00%	+£80.96
Michael Attwater/William	37	2	5.41%	+£72.45

Carson				
Phil McEntee/Callum Shepherd	20	4	20.00%	+£69.66

Profit or Loss backing the unnamed favourite – non-handicaps

Runners	Winners	Strike Rate	Profit/Loss to BSP
1086	451	41.53%	-£32.44-

Profit or Loss backing the unnamed favourite – handicaps

Runners	Winners	Strike Rate	Profit/Loss to BSP
2821	858	30.41%	+£92.89

Profit or loss backing the unnamed second favourite - non-handicaps

Runners	Winners	Strike Rate	Profit/Loss to BSP
1034	236	22.82%	-£3.97

Profit or loss backing the unnamed second favourite - handicaps

Runners	Winners	Strike Rate	Profit/Loss to BSP
2707	514	18.99%	-£92.90

Profit or Loss backing horses who won last time out - non-handicaps

Runners	Winners	Strike Rate	Profit/Loss to BSP
365	106	29.04%	-£38.63

Profit or Loss backing horses who won last time out - handicaps

Runners	Winners	Strike Rate	Profit/Loss to BSP
2672	516	19.31%	-£120.17

Profit or loss backing Top-Weights in handicaps

Runners	Winners	Strike Rate	Profit/Loss to BSP
3231	483	14.95%	-£321.09

Most profitable sires – non- handicaps

Zoffany	74	8	10.81%	+£173.50
Lope De Vega	68	19	27.94%	+£122.19
The Gurkha	15	6	40.00%	+£117.63
Mount Nelson	27	3	11.11%	+£114.58
Azamour	16	7	43.75%	+£76.80

Most profitable sires – handicaps

Kodiac	595	67	11.26%	+£230.05
Cityscape	59	9	15.25%	+£221,70
Oasis Dream	287	40	13.94%	+£190.90
Holy Roman Emperor	148	24	16.22%	+£164.93
Firebreak	43	5	11.63%	+£163.99

Dundalk

Top jockeys by Strike Rate – non-handicaps

Name Of Jockey	Rides	Winners	Strike Rate	Profit/Loss to BSP
Ryan Moore	10	6	60.00%	+£4.84
Daniel King	23	5	21.74%	+£38.20
Dean Curran	16	3	18.75%	-£7.61
L P Dempsey	27	5	18.52%	+£1.98
Colin Keane	624	104	16.67%	-£39.79

Top jockeys by Strike Rate – handicaps

Name Of Jockey	Rides	Winners	Strike Rate	Profit/Loss to BSP
Ciara Flynn	17	4	23.53%	+£27.57
Colin Keane	912	126	13.82%	+£44.86
Ronan Whelan	662	90	13.60%	+£182.19
John Egan	55	7	12.73%	-£9.87
Sam Ewing	178	22	12.36%	+£30.05

Top jockeys by Profit – non-handicaps

Name Of Jockey	Rides	Winners	Strike Rate	Profit/Loss to BSP
Oisin Orr	178	18	10.11%	+£319.81
Connor King	194	14	7.22%	+£274.38
James Ryan	23	2	8.70%	+£148.88
Conor Hoban	350	26	7.43%	+£113.12
Seamie Heffernan	408	51	12.50%	+£71.84

Top jockeys by Profit – handicaps

Name Of Jockey	Rides	Winners	Strike Rate	Profit/Loss to BSP
Killian Hennessy	51	2	3.92%	+£202.05
Ross Coakley	474	41	8.65%	+£191.91
Ronan Whelan	662	90	13.60%	+£182.19

Conor Hoban	762	85	11.15%	+£169.32
Alan Persse	172	9	5.24%	+£164.28

Top trainers by Strike Rate – non-handicaps

Name Of Trainer	Runners	Winners	Strike Rate	Profit/Loss to BSP
Sir Mark Prescott Bt	10	5	50.00%	+£2.74
P Twomey	19	8	42.11%	+£118.89
A P O'Brien	390	109	27.95%	-£12.84
Noel Kelly	16	4	25.00%	+£27.15
Donnacha O'Brien	34	8	23.53%	+£8.27

Top trainers by Strike Rate – handicaps

Name Of Trainer	Runners	Winners	Strike Rate	Profit/Loss to BSP
Donnacha O'Brien	11	3	27.27%	+£7.54
Tony Carroll	11	3	27.27%	+£4.94
John E Kiely	15	4	26.67%	+£20.23
Donal Commins	12	3	25.00%	+£162.11
Ellmarie Holden	12	3	25.00%	+£26.92

Top trainers by Profit – non-handicaps

Name Of Trainer	Runners	Winners	Strike Rate	Profit/Loss to BSP
Andrew Oliver	212	23	10.85%	+£251.59
Denis W Cullen	37	2	5.41%	+£190.31
P Twomey	19	8	42.11%	+£118.89
Jack W Davison	55	6	10.91%	+£109.16
Shane Donohoe	44	4	9.09%	+£99.12

Top trainers by Profit – handicaps

Name Of Trainer	Runners	Winners	Strike Rate	Profit/Loss to BSP
Lee Smyth	234	19	8.12%	+£417.10
John James Feane	358	40	11.17%	+£316.41

Liam Lennon	33	1	3.03%	+£285.42
Eamonn O'Connell	75	6	8.00%	+£200.76
Anthony McCann	422	30	7.11%	+£192.31

Top trainer/jockey combos by Strike Rate – non-handicaps

Name of Trainer/Jockey	Qualifiers	Winners	Strike Rate	Profit/Loss to BSP
A P O'Brien/Ryan Moore	10	6	60.00%	+£4.84
Henry De Bromhead/ Billy Lee	14	5	35.71%	+£27.22
P Twomey/Billy Lee	15	5	33.33%	+£83.39
A P O'Brien/Seamie Heffernan	98	32	32.65%	-£0.46
Donnacha O'Brien/Gavin Ryan	25	8	32.00%	+£17.23

Top trainer/jockey combos by Strike Rate – handicaps

Name of Trainer/Jockey	Qualifiers	Winners	Strike Rate	Profit/Loss to BSP
M Halford/Colin Keane	10	5	50.00%	+£12.88
Conor O'Dwyer/Billy Lee	17	7	41.18%	+£15.33
Ms Sheila Lavery/Gary Carroll	13	5	38.46%	+£19.78
Andrew Oliver/Ronan Whelan	14	5	35.71%	+£53.18
Matthew J Smith/Sam Ewing	15	5	33.33%	+£7.70

Top trainer/jockey combos by Profit – non-handicaps

Name of Trainer/Jockey	Qualifiers	Winners	Strike Rate	Profit/Loss to BSP
Andrew Oliver/Conor Hoban	33	6	18.18%	+£280.00
T G McCourt/James Ryan	11	1	9.09%	+£155.62
P Twomey/Billy Lee	15	5	33.33%	+£83.39
John Joseph Murphy/Connor King	14	2	14.29%	+£55.83
Ger Lyons/Gary Carroll	107	17	15.89%	+£53.03

Top trainer/jockey combos by Profit – handicaps

Name of Trainer/Jockey	Qualifiers	Winners	Strike Rate	Profit/Loss to BSP
John Joseph Murphy/Colin Keane	25	5	20.00%	+£125.73
Richard John O'Brien/Scott McCullagh	11	2	18.18%	+£102.31
Damian Joseph English/Rory Cleary	132	14	10.61%	+£94.87
Luke Comer/Chris Hayes	45	8	17.78%	+£78.21
Lee Smyth/Shane Kelly	12	2	16.67%	+£70.13

Profit or Loss backing the unnamed favourite – non-handicaps

Runners	Winners	Strike Rate	Profit/Loss to BSP

1587	632	39.82£	+£21.74

Profit or Loss backing the unnamed favourite – handicaps

Runners	Winners	Strike Rate	Profit/Loss to BSP
2731	660	24.17%	+£1.99

Profit or loss backing the unnamed second favourite - non-handicaps

Runners	Winners	Strike Rate	Profit/Loss to BSP
1527	314	20.56%	-£97.84

Profit or loss backing the unnamed second favourite - handicaps

Runners	Winners	Strike Rate	Profit/Loss to BSP
2502	443	17.71%	+£70.15

Profit or Loss backing horses who won last time out - non-handicaps

Runners	Winners	Strike Rate	Profit/Loss to BSP
593	125	21.08%	-£60.42

Profit or Loss backing horses who won last time out - handicaps

Runners	Winners	Strike Rate	Profit/Loss to BSP
2456	420	17.10%	+£303.86

Profit or loss backing Top-Weights in handicaps

Runners	Winners	Strike Rate	Profit/Loss to BSP
2828	386	13.65%	-£41.15

Most profitable sires – non- handicaps

Camacho	208	14	6.73%	+£326.30
Lawman	239	20	8.37%	+£227.32
Elzaam	148	22	14.86%	+£226.45

| Free Eagle | 33 | 3 | 9.09% | +£206.24 |
| Verglas | 147 | 24 | 16.33% | +£162.08 |

Most profitable sires – handicaps

Elzaam	112	9	8.04%	+£250.00
Bushranger	81	8	9.88%	+£230.62
Famous Name	27	2	7.41%	+£216.72
Archipenko	14	4	28.57%	+£202.05
Markaz	11	1	9.09%	+£155.62

Kempton

Top jockeys by Strike Rate – non-handicaps

Name Of Jockey	Rides	Winners	Strike Rate	Profit/Loss to BSP
Benoit de la Sayette	16	6	37.50%	+£60.96
Danny Tudhope	24	7	29.17%	+£29.19
Frankie Dettori	69	18	26.09%	-£17.09
William Buick	311	80	25.72%	-£4.20
James Doyle	329	81	24.62%	+£1.29

Top jockeys by Strike Rate – handicaps

Name Of Jockey	Rides	Winners	Strike Rate	Profit/Loss to BSP
Joanna Mason	15	5	33.33%	+£18.53
Benoit de la Sayette	25	6	24.00%	-£1.45
Pat Dobbs	35	8	22.86%	+£76.66
William Buick	319	64	20.06%	-£58.78
Serena Brotherton	10	2	20.00%	+£1.89

Top jockeys by Profit – non-handicaps

Name Of Jockey	Rides	Winners	Strike Rate	Profit/Loss to BSP
Daniel Muscutt	213	22	10.33%	+£461.21
Richard Kingscote	283	41	14.49%	+£261.25
Andrea Atzeni	267	55	20.60%	+£158.49
Sam Hitchcott	49	2	4.08%	+£129.59
Dylan Hogan	40	1	2.50%	+£87.42

Top jockeys by Profit – handicaps

Name Of Jockey	Rides	Winners	Strike Rate	Profit/Loss to BSP
Pat Cosgrave	401	51	12.72%	+£182.81

Martin Dwyer	401	47	11.72%	+£158.18
Daniel Muscutt	424	47	11.08%	+£146.72
Andrea Atzeni	288	42	14.58%	+£121.14
John Egan	272	17	6.25%	+£118.29

Top trainers by Strike Rate – non-handicaps

Name Of Trainer	Runners	Winners	Strike Rate	Profit/Loss to BSP
Charlie Appleby	324	95	29.32%	+£10.34
Saeed bin Suroor	237	65	27.43%	+£32.53
John Gosden	591	140	23.69%	+£13.59
Roger Varian	336	75	22.32%	+£50.43
Archie Watson	135	28	20.74%	+£2.86

Top trainers by Strike Rate – handicaps

Name Of Trainer	Runners	Winners	Strike Rate	Profit/Loss to BSP
Harry Eustace	15	5	33.33%	+£19.89
Charlie Appleby	107	33	30.84%	+£8.12
Simon and Ed Crisford	35	10	28.57%	+£25.05
Julie Camacho	38	10	26.32%	+£96.33
Kevin Phillipart de Foy	58	14	24.14%	+£6.69

Top trainers by Profit – non-handicaps

Name Of Trainer	Runners	Winners	Strike Rate	Profit/Loss to BSP
Jonathan Portman	149	8	5.37%	+£515.44
Andrew Balding	465	64	13.76%	+£208.58
J S Moore	101	8	7.92%	+£155.32
Roger Charlton	276	39	14.13%	+£140.32
Clive Cox	250	31	12.40%	+£125.27

Top trainers by Profit – handicaps

Name Of Trainer	Runners	Winners	Strike Rate	Profit/Loss to BSP

Mark Rimell	55	20	18.18%	+£150.31
John Ryan	204	18	8.82%	+£136.34
Martin Smith	66	8	12.12%	+£133.62
John E Long	134	10	7.46%	+£130.74
Simon Dow	366	33	9.02%	+£123.96

Top trainer/jockey combos by Strike Rate – non-handicaps

Name of Trainer/Jockey	Qualifiers	Winners	Strike Rate	Profit/Loss to BSP
John Gosden/Jim Crowley	16	9	56.25%	+£15.06
John Gosden/Paul Hanagan	15	6	40.00%	+£16.93
Saeed bin Suroor/Oisin Murphy	25	10	40.00%	+£10.81
Simon and Ed Crisford/James Doyle	15	6	40.00%	+£7.66
Charlie Appleby/James Doyle	46	18	39.13%	+£1.20

Top trainer/jockey combos by Strike Rate – handicaps

Name of Trainer/Jockey	Qualifiers	Winners	Strike Rate	Profit/Loss to BSP
Charlie Appleby/William Buick	389	16	41.03%	+£6.10
Mark Rimell/Tom Marquand	15	6	40.00%	+£174.08
Michael Blake/Richard Kingscote	14	5	35.71%	+£48.07
Saeed bin Suroor/Frankie Dettori	17	6	35.29%	+£4.33
Ralph	17	6	35.29%	+£42.11

Beckett/Oisin Murphy				

Top trainer/jockey combos by Profit – non-handicaps

Name of Trainer/Jockey	Qualifiers	Winners	Strike Rate	Profit/Loss to BSP
Andrew Balding/David Probert	182	27	14.84%	+£220.66
Roger Charlton/Kieran Shoemark	42	6	14.29%	+£125.87
Richard Hughes/Finley Marsh	12	3	25.00%	+£68.46
Hughie Morrison/Liam Keniry	20	3	15.00%	+£46.44
Roger Varian/Dane O'Neill	13	3	23.08%	+£45.65

Top trainer/jockey combos by Profit – handicaps

Name of Trainer/Jockey	Qualifiers	Winners	Strike Rate	Profit/Loss to BSP
Simon Dow/John Egan	26	3	11.54%	+£185.31
Mark Rimell/Tom Marquand	15	6	40.00%	+£174.08
Seamus Durack/Shane Kelly	12	1	8.33%	+£111.44
William Muir/Martin Dwyer	99	12	12.12%	+£103.15
Stuart Williams/Andrea Atzeni	13	3	23.08%	+£102.37

Profit or Loss backing the unnamed favourite – non-handicaps

Runners	Winners	Strike Rate	Profit/Loss to BSP
3091	1199	38.79%	-£90.12

Profit or Loss backing the unnamed favourite – handicaps

Runners	Winners	Strike Rate	Profit/Loss to BSP
6456	1788	27.70%	-£70.23

Profit or loss backing the unnamed second favourite - non-handicaps

Runners	Winners	Strike Rate	Profit/Loss to BSP
2954	663	22.44%	+£149.53

Profit or loss backing the unnamed second favourite - handicaps

Runners	Winners	Strike Rate	Profit/Loss to BSP
6086	1071	17.60%	-£308.94

Profit or Loss backing horses who won last time out - non-handicaps

Runners	Winners	Strike Rate	Profit/Loss to BSP
1130	281	24.87%	-£141.51

Profit or Loss backing horses who won last time out - handicaps

Runners	Winners	Strike Rate	Profit/Loss to BSP
6685	1226	18.34%	+£101.51

Profit or loss backing Top-Weights in handicaps

Runners	Winners	Strike Rate	Profit/Loss to BSP
8558	1149	13.43%	-£523.46

Most profitable sires – non- handicaps

Big Bad Bob	50	3	6.00%	+£508.74
Exceed And Excel	240	43	17.92%	+£301.04
Diamond Green	14	1	7.14%	+£196.86
Monsieur Bond	40	6	15.00%	+£158.21
Singspiel	28	7	25.00%	+£154.27

Most profitable sires – handicaps

Ivawood	36	5	13.89%	+£187.63
Dutch Art	415	47	11.33%	+£186.28
Cable Bay	105	9	8.57%	+£162.30
Shamardal	325	61	18.77%	+£147.83
Zamindar	170	20	11.76%	+£134.59

Lingfield

Top jockeys by Strike Rate – non-handicaps

Name Of Jockey	Rides	Winners	Strike Rate	Profit/Loss to BSP
Frankie Dettori	68	27	39.71%	+£25.76
Ryan Moore	179	64	35.75%	+£54.64
Shane Gray	20	7	35.00%	+£1.15
David Nolan	12	3	25.00%	+£11.64
James Doyle	172	43	25.00%	+£41.36

Top jockeys by Strike Rate – handicaps

Name Of Jockey	Rides	Winners	Strike Rate	Profit/Loss to BSP
Ryan Moore	185	47	25.41%	-£8.76
Connor Beasley	24	6	25.00%	+£10.60
Mr Simon Walker	25	6	24.00%	+£5.07
Mohammed Tabti	13	3	23.08%	+£123.90
Andrea Atzeni	219	47	21.46%	+£158.17

Top jockeys by Profit – non-handicaps

Name Of Jockey	Rides	Winners	Strike Rate	Profit/Loss to BSP
Liam Keniry	313	27	8.63%	+£312.38
Jack Mitchell	136	29	21.32%	+£90.23
Jimmy Quinn	100	9	9.00%	+£80.14
Joey Haynes	102	4	3.92%	+£61.11
Jim Crowley	358	75	20.95%	+£55.74

Top jockeys by Profit – handicaps

Name Of Jockey	Rides	Winners	Strike Rate	Profit/Loss to BSP
John Fahy	159	18	11.32%	+£193.66
Andrea Atzeni	219	47	21.46%	+£158.17
Joe Fanning	447	79	17.67%	+£145.07

Mohammed Tabti	13	3	23.08%	+£123.90
Darragh Keenan	238	36	15.13%	+£120.62

Top trainers by Strike Rate – non-handicaps

Name Of Trainer	Runners	Winners	Strike Rate	Profit/Loss to BSP
Sean Curran	24	8	33.33%	-£2.57
Sir Michael Stoute	118	37	31.36%	+£71.77
Charlie Appleby	160	49	30.63%	+£33.43
Geoff Oldroyd	10	3	30.00%	+£15.38
William Haggas	241	65	26.97%	-£8.23

Top trainers by Strike Rate – handicaps

Name Of Trainer	Runners	Winners	Strike Rate	Profit/Loss to BSP
Jeremy Scott	15	5	33.33%	+£24.59
Charlie Appleby	70	23	32.86%	+£12.02
Saeed bin Suroor	68	22	32.35%	+£16.01
Neil King	32	10	31.25%	+£38.64
Sir Michael Stoute	50	15	30.00%	+£41.29

Top trainers by Profit – non-handicaps

Name Of Trainer	Runners	Winners	Strike Rate	Profit/Loss to BSP
Jonathan Portman	110	11	10.00%	+£486.02
Mark Usher	53	2	3.77%	+£358.93
Michael Madgwick	28	2	7.14%	+£292.62
J S Moore	199	17	8.54%	+£191.60
Jimmy Fox	12	1	8.33%	+£150.64

Top trainers by Profit – handicaps

Name Of Trainer	Runners	Winners	Strike Rate	Profit/Loss to BSP

John Gallagher	92	10	10.87%	+£103.39
Jimmy Fox	93	5	5.38%	+£101.20
Mark Hoad	136	10	7.35%	+£97.59
Suzy Smith	11	1	9.09%	+£96.91
Julia Feilden	171	22	12.87%	+£96.57

Top trainer/jockey combos by Strike Rate – non-handicaps

Name of Trainer/Jockey	Qualifiers	Winners	Strike Rate	Profit/Loss to BSP
Charlie Appleby/Shane Gray	10	6	60.00%	+£6.89
Sir Michael Stoute/Ryan Moore	45	23	51.11%	+£61.71
David Simcock/Jim Crowley	22	11	50.00%	+£44.98
Henry Candy/Dane O'Neill	10	5	50.00%	+£17.68
Saeed bin Suroor/James Doyle	15	7	46.67%	+£7.29

Top trainer/jockey combos by Strike Rate – handicaps

Name of Trainer/Jockey	Qualifiers	Winners	Strike Rate	Profit/Loss to BSP
Denis Coakley/George Bass	10	6	60.00%	+£62.14
William Haggas/Tom Marquand	14	7	50.00%	+£16.63
Charlie Appleby/Adam Kirby	20	10	50.00%	+£15.62
Daniel and Claire Kubler/Richard Kingscote	11	5	45.45%	+£9.12
Ralph	22	10	45.45%	+£32.75

Beckett/Jim Crowley				

Top trainer/jockey combos by Profit – non-handicaps

Name of Trainer/Jockey	Qualifiers	Winners	Strike Rate	Profit/Loss to BSP
Mark Usher/Liam Keniry	14	2	14.29%	+£397.93
Andrew Balding/David Probert	110	21	19.09%	+£86.64
Sir Michael Stoute/Ryan Moore	45	23	51.11%	+£61.71
Roger Varian/Jack Mitchell	44	13	29.55%	+£54.99
William Muir/Martin Dwyer	38	7	18.42%	+£53.78

Top trainer/jockey combos by Profit – handicaps

Name of Trainer/Jockey	Qualifiers	Winners	Strike Rate	Profit/Loss to BSP
John Gallagher/Darragh Keenan	13	3	23.08%	+£113.92
Dean Ivory/George Downing	21	3	14.29%	+£91.20
Ali Stronge/Tom Marquand	18	4	22.22%	+£85.94
Richard Hannon/Sean Levey	112	19	16.96%	+£67.09
Denis Coakley/George Bass	10	6	60.00%	+£62.14

Profit or Loss backing the unnamed favourite – non-handicaps

Runners	Winners	Strike Rate	Profit/Loss to BSP
4501	1740	38.66%	-£22.75

Profit or Loss backing the unnamed favourite – handicaps

Runners	Winners	Strike Rate	Profit/Loss to BSP
6952	1978	28.45%	+£77.32

Profit or loss backing the unnamed second favourite - non-handicaps

Runners	Winners	Strike Rate	Profit/Loss to BSP
4231	912	21.56%	+£33.08

Profit or loss backing the unnamed second favourite - handicaps

Runners	Winners	Strike Rate	Profit/Loss to BSP
6512	1185	18.20%	-£213.46

Profit or Loss backing horses who won last time out - non-handicaps

Runners	Winners	Strike Rate	Profit/Loss to BSP
19342	424	21.95%	-£185.97

Profit or Loss backing horses who won last time out - handicaps

Runners	Winners	Strike Rate	Profit/Loss to BSP
6964	1340	19.24%	+£17.96

Profit or loss backing Top-Weights in handicaps

Runners	Winners	Strike Rate	Profit/Loss to BSP
8310	1275	15.34%	-£181.89

Most profitable sires – non- handicaps

Excellent Art	79	12	15.19%	+£496.66
Approve	42	7	16.67%	+£395.54
Multiplex	39	5	12.82%	+£309.57
Mount Nelson	85	8	9.41%	+£308.97
Dandy Man	77	11	14.29%	+£156.59

Most profitable sires – handicaps

Mujahid	35	3	8.57%	+£148.52
Sixties Icon	147	9	6.12%	+£129.30
Medicean	204	30	14.71%	+£127.59
Byron	223	30	13.45%	+£124.57
Delegator	114	18	15.79%	+£111.08

Newcastle

Top jockeys by Strike Rate – non-handicaps

Name Of Jockey	Rides	Winners	Strike Rate	Profit/Loss to BSP
Jim Crowley	30	14	46.67%	+£5.40
Robert Havlin	89	31	34.83%	-£8.21
James Doyle	23	8	34.78%	-£0.34
William Buick	12	4	33.33%	+£4.30
David Probert	26	8	30.77%	+£8.57

Top jockeys by Strike Rate – handicaps

Name Of Jockey	Rides	Winners	Strike Rate	Profit/Loss to BSP
Hector Crouch	11	3	27.27%	+£2.38
James Doyle	27	7	25.93%	-£2.42
Christian Howarth	12	3	25.00%	+£8.26
Oisin Murphy	64	15	23.44%	+£40.32
Laura Pearson	39	9	23.08%	+£41.00

Top jockeys by Profit – non-handicaps

Name Of Jockey	Rides	Winners	Strike Rate	Profit/Loss to BSP
Ben Curtis	179	39	21.79%	+£225.97
P J McDonald	256	38	14.84%	+£92.81
Joe Fanning	146	24	16.44%	+£88.69
Barry McHugh	77	5	6.49%	+£46.98
Ben Robinson	101	8	7.92%	+£46.90

Top jockeys by Profit – handicaps

Name Of Jockey	Rides	Winners	Strike Rate	Profit/Loss to BSP
Shane Gray	271	22	8.12%	+£318.49
James Sullivan	527	39	7.40%	+£217.13
Phil Dennis	490	42	8.57%	+£174.01
Joanna Mason	111	13	11.71%	+£169.44

Saffie Osborne	27	5	18.52%	+£127.02

Top trainers by Strike Rate – non-handicaps

Name Of Trainer	Runners	Winners	Strike Rate	Profit/Loss to BSP
Roger Charlton	16	8	50.00%	+£6.05
Richard Spencer	13	6	46.15%	+£23.30
Heather Main	13	5	38.46%	+£62.95
Charlie Appleby	49	17	34.69%	+£2.38
Simon and Ed Crisford	29	10	34.48%	+£8.24

Top trainers by Strike Rate – handicaps

Name Of Trainer	Runners	Winners	Strike Rate	Profit/Loss to BSP
Sir Michael Stoute	30	11	36.67%	+£31.71
William Haggas	65	21	32.31%	+£4.63
Ralph Beckett	22	7	31.82%	+£16.80
George Boughey	58	16	27.59%	+£24.25
Saeed bin Suroor	51	14	27.45%	+£1.87

Top trainers by Profit – non-handicaps

Name Of Trainer	Runners	Winners	Strike Rate	Profit/Loss to BSP
Chris Fairhurst	21	5	23.81%	+£235.48
K R Burke	226	33	14.60%	+£227.69
Michael Easterby	64	2	3.13%	+£112.19
Henry Spiller	10	2	20.00%	+£86.00
Heather Main	13	5	38.46%	+£62.95

Top trainers by Profit – handicaps

Name Of Trainer	Runners	Winners	Strike Rate	Profit/Loss to BSP
Tom Tate	90	14	15.56%	+£322.75
Jim Goldie	555	59	10.63%	+£155.56
Phillip Makin	109	9	8.26%	+£128.53

Richard Fahey	699	95	13.59%	+£117.04
Jamie Osborne	26	3	11.54%	+£102.45

Top trainer/jockey combos by Strike Rate – non-handicaps

Name of Trainer/Jockey	Qualifiers	Winners	Strike Rate	Profit/Loss to BSP
Simon and Ed Crisford/Jack Mitchell	11	5	45.45%	-£0.98
William Haggas/Ben Curtis	14	6	42.86%	+£18.72
Michael Dods/Callum Rodriguez	20	8	40.00%	+£37.82
Archie Watson/Hollie Doyle	23	9	39.13%	+£9.61
Hugo Palmer/Josephine Gordon	26	10	38.46%	+£31.17

Top trainer/jockey combos by Strike Rate – handicaps

Name of Trainer/Jockey	Qualifiers	Winners	Strike Rate	Profit/Loss to BSP
Oliver Greenall and Josh Guerriero/Kevin Stott	13	5	38.46%	+£12.91
Marco Botti/Daniel Muscutt	13	5	38.46%	+£20.72
Andrew Balding/David Probert	13	5	38.46%	+£15.47
Michael Wigham/Joe Fanning	11	4	36.36%	+£28.02
David Evans/Andrew Mullen	12	4	33.33%	+£32.21

Top trainer/jockey combos by Profit – non-handicaps

Name of Trainer/Jockey	Qualifiers	Winners	Strike Rate	Profit/Loss to BSP
Karl Burke/Ben Curtis	39	13	33.33%	+£226.33
Mark Johnston/Joe Fanning	83	9	10.84%	+£70.02
Alan Brown/Dale Swift	12	2	16.67%	+£58.63
Brian Ellison/Ben Robinson	65	5	7.69%	+£49.71
Tim Easterby/Duran Fentiman	26	2	7.69%	+£40.68

Top trainer/jockey combos by Profit – handicaps

Name of Trainer/Jockey	Qualifiers	Winners	Strike Rate	Profit/Loss to BSP
Tom Tate/James Sullivan	31	4	12.90%	+£259.89
Ann Duffield/Shane Gray	37	4	10.81%	+£158.79
Jim Goldie/Phil Dennis	134	19	14.18%	+£154.84
Tom Tate/Andrew Mullen	30	9	30.00%	+£74.21
Ben Haslam/Andrew Mullen	119	21	17.65%	+£71.84

Profit or Loss backing the unnamed favourite – non-handicaps

Runners	Winners	Strike Rate	Profit/Loss to BSP
718	306	42.62%	-£22.97

Profit or Loss backing the unnamed favourite – handicaps

Runners	Winners	Strike Rate	Profit/Loss to BSP
2079	564	27.13%	-£86.08

Profit or loss backing the unnamed second favourite - non-handicaps

Runners	Winners	Strike Rate	Profit/Loss to BSP
7121	157	22.05%	-£30.77

Profit or loss backing the unnamed second favourite - handicaps

Runners	Winners	Strike Rate	Profit/Loss to BSP
1938	347	17.91%	-£34.49

Profit or Loss backing horses who won last time out - non-handicaps

Runners	Winners	Strike Rate	Profit/Loss to BSP
330	91	27.58%	-£0.01

Profit or Loss backing horses who won last time out - handicaps

Runners	Winners	Strike Rate	Profit/Loss to BSP
1932	343	17.75%	-£16.44

Profit or loss backing Top-Weights in handicaps

Runners	Winners	Strike Rate	Profit/Loss to BSP
2437	352	14.44%	+£194.80

Most profitable sires – non- handicaps

Bahamian Bounty	18	1	5.56%	+£171.04
Lethal Force	42	4	9.52%	+£139.33
Showcasing	76	9	11.84%	+£136.78

| Harbour Watch | 50 | 4 | 8.00% | +£133.58 |
| Mukhadram | 29 | 6 | 20.69% | +£79.63 |

Most profitable sires – handicaps

Dandy Man	379	38	10.03%	+£191.33
Poet's Voice	161	11	6.83%	+£184.46
Zoffany	203	28	13.79%	+£182.95
Swiss Spirit	129	17	13.18%	+£129.27
Stimulation	49	3	6.12%	+£116.69

Southwell

Top jockeys by Strike Rate – non-handicaps

Name Of Jockey	Rides	Winners	Strike Rate	Profit/Loss to BSP
Danny Tudhope	56	22	39.29%	+£60.07
Jamie Spencer	18	7	38.89%	-£4.33
Neil Callan	15	5	33.33%	+£16.03
Oisin Murphy	36	12	33.33%	-£0.01
Joshua Bryan	12	4	33.33%	-£2.65

Top jockeys by Strike Rate – handicaps

Name Of Jockey	Rides	Winners	Strike Rate	Profit/Loss to BSP
George Buckell	16	7	42.75%	+£26.33
Mr Patrick Millman	14	4	28.57%	+£17.44
Sean Levey	47	12	25.53%	+£62.82
Mr Simon Walker	28	7	25.00%	-£1.16
Pat Cosgrave	12	3	25.00%	+£44.62

Top jockeys by Profit – non-handicaps

Name Of Jockey	Rides	Winners	Strike Rate	Profit/Loss to BSP
James Sullivan	63	7	11.11%	+£325.46
George Downing	10	2	20.00%	+£185.55
Joey Haynes	62	8	12.90%	+£113.46
Barry McHugh	77	15	18.48%	+£70.57
Tony Hamilton	74	15	20.27%	+£67.61

Top jockeys by Profit – handicaps

Name Of Jockey	Rides	Winners	Strike Rate	Profit/Loss to BSP
Kieran O'Neill	452	46	10.18%	+£529.56
Ben Curtis	406	79	19.46%	+£231.44
Franny Norton	148	17	11.49%	+£194.75

Callum Rodriguez	108	16	14.81%	+£175.01
Ben Sanderson	48	9	18.75%	+£133.27

Top trainers by Strike Rate – non-handicaps

Name Of Trainer	Runners	Winners	Strike Rate	Profit/Loss to BSP
William Haggas	21	11	52.38%	+£8.87
Charlie Appleby	11	5	45.45%	+£2.95
Richard Hughes	26	10	38.46%	+£11.28
Saeed bin Suroor	17	6	35.29%	-£1.24
George Boughey	24	8	33.33%	-£2.49

Top trainers by Strike Rate – handicaps

Name Of Trainer	Runners	Winners	Strike Rate	Profit/Loss to BSP
James Fanshawe	15	6	40.00%	+£30.35
Brett Johnson	11	4	36.36%	+£11.12
James Ferguson	11	4	36.36%	-£0.01
William Knight	12	4	33.33%	+£18.93
David Simcock	34	11	32.35%	+£30.19

Top trainers by Profit – non-handicaps

Name Of Trainer	Runners	Winners	Strike Rate	Profit/Loss to BSP
Karl Burke	120	30	25.00%	+£196.63
Tony Carroll	37	6	16.22%	+£173.62
Michael Bell	28	5	17.86%	+£82.32
Robert Cowell	58	7	12.07%	+£55.70
Ollie Pears	30	5	16.67%	+£49.61

Top trainers by Profit – handicaps

Name Of Trainer	Runners	Winners	Strike Rate	Profit/Loss to BSP
Scott Dixon	997	84	8.43%	+£482.08
Derek Shaw	450	54	12.00%	+£241.02
Karl Burke	251	41	16.33%	+£159.13
Roger Fell	200	26	13.00%	+£154.47

| Tim Easterby | 219 | 33 | 15.07% | +£149.35 |

Top trainer/jockey combos by Strike Rate – non-handicaps

Name of Trainer/Jockey	Qualifiers	Winners	Strike Rate	Profit/Loss to BSP
Richard Hughes/Shane Kelly	12	8	66.67%	+£21.78
Karl Burke/Joey Haynes	14	7	50.00%	+£155.56
Archie Watson/Luke Morris	11	5	45.45%	+£9.77
Derek Shaw/Dale Swift	10	4	40.00%	+£12.61
Mark Johnston/Joe Fanning	68	25	36.76%	+£7.65

Top trainer/jockey combos by Strike Rate – handicaps

Name of Trainer/Jockey	Qualifiers	Winners	Strike Rate	Profit/Loss to BSP
Lawrence Mullaney/William Carver	10	5	50.00%	+£7.38
Tony Carroll/Aled Beech	11	5	45.45%	+£68.57
Mike Murphy and Michael Keady/Daniel Muscutt	24	10	41.67%	+£23.87
Philip Kirby/Ben Curtis	10	4	40.00%	+£10.07
George Boughey/Mark Crehan	10	4	40.00%	+£0.84

Top trainer/jockey combos by Profit – non-handicaps

Name of Trainer/Jockey	Qualifiers	Winners	Strike Rate	Profit/Loss to BSP

Karl Burke/Joey Haynes	14	7	50.00%	+£155.56
Tony Coyle/Barry McHugh	20	3	15.00%	+£37.31
Anthony Carson/William Carson	12	3	25.00%	+£37.20
Michael Appleby/Andrew Mullen	59	10	16.95%	+£26.51
Robert Cowell/Luke Morris	11	2	18.18%	+£26.10

Top trainer/jockey combos by Profit – handicaps

Name of Trainer/Jockey	Qualifiers	Winners	Strike Rate	Profit/Loss to BSP
Scott Dixon/Kieran O'Neill	215	26	12.09%	+£515.54
Michael Dods/Callum Rodriguez	12	2	16.67%	+£159.02
Roger Fell/Ben Sanderson	34	7	20.59%	+£129.40
Michale Mullineaux/Robert Havlin	10	3	30.00%	+£105.23
Nigel Tinkler/Faye McManoman	10	1	10.00%	+£97.82

Profit or Loss backing the unnamed favourite – non-handicaps

Runners	Winners	Strike Rate	Profit/Loss to BSP
2718	1047	38.52%	+£56.88

Profit or Loss backing the unnamed favourite – handicaps

Runners	Winners	Strike Rate	Profit/Loss to BSP
4875	1412	28.96%	-£133.61

Profit or loss backing the unnamed second favourite - non-handicaps

Runners	Winners	Strike Rate	Profit/Loss to BSP
2620	559	21.34%	+£4.75

Profit or loss backing the unnamed second favourite - handicaps

Runners	Winners	Strike Rate	Profit/Loss to BSP
4559	845	18.53%	-£173.89

Profit or Loss backing horses who won last time out - non-handicaps

Runners	Winners	Strike Rate	Profit/Loss to BSP
932	252	27.04%	-£28.21

Profit or Loss backing horses who won last time out - handicaps

Runners	Winners	Strike Rate	Profit/Loss to BSP
4531	934	20.61%	-£285.64

Profit or loss backing Top-Weights in handicaps

Runners	Winners	Strike Rate	Profit/Loss to BSP
5507	884	16.05%	-£205.13

Most profitable sires – non- handicaps

Fasliyev	11	2	18.18%	+£152.93
Misu Bond	21	3	14.29%	+£141.54
Fast Company	35	4	11.43%	+£140.04
Paco Boy	17	5	29.41%	+£112.36
Baltic King	20	8	40.00%	+£87.75

Most profitable sires – handicaps

Aussie Rules	51	2	3.92%	+£416.22
Smart Strike	39	10	25.64%	+£231.11

Brazen Beau	43	6	13.95%	+£161.68
Kodiac	305	30	9.84%	+£129.69
Dream Ahead	81	7	8.64%	+£119.58

Wolverhampton

Top jockeys by Strike Rate – non-handicaps

Name Of Jockey	Rides	Winners	Strike Rate	Profit/Loss to BSP
Ryan Moore	27	11	40.74%	+£10.71
Mickael Barzalona	16	6	37.50%	+£6.77
James Doyle	118	44	37.29%	+£59.62
William Buick	63	22	34.92%	+£9.61
Adam Kirby	312	91	29.17%	+£8.08

Top jockeys by Strike Rate – handicaps

Name Of Jockey	Rides	Winners	Strike Rate	Profit/Loss to BSP
Ryan Moore	34	14	41.18%	+£14.65
Mr Simon Walker	70	18	25.71%	-£5.47
Jim Crowley	157	40	25.48%	+£57.23
Benoit de la Sayette	28	7	25.00%	+£20.61
Rose Dawes	12	3	25.00%	+£8.16

Top jockeys by Profit – non-handicaps

Name Of Jockey	Rides	Winners	Strike Rate	Profit/Loss to BSP
Duran Fentiman	45	2	4.44%	+£168.75
Phil Dennis	59	2	3.39%	+£133.51
Stefano Cherchi	53	4	7.55%	+£128.50
Gina Mangan	25	4	16.00%	+£112.34
David Nolan	51	9	17.65%	+£103.94

Top jockeys by Profit – handicaps

Name Of Jockey	Rides	Winners	Strike Rate	Profit/Loss to BSP
Stevie Donohoe	623	75	12.04%	+£350.01
Raul Da Silva	272	31	11.40%	+£271.86

Rob Hornby	385	36	9.35%	+£205.79
Dale Swift	263	28	10.65%	+£174.61
Ben Robinson	199	20	10.05%	+£170.99

Top trainers by Strike Rate – non-handicaps

Name Of Trainer	Runners	Winners	Strike Rate	Profit/Loss to BSP
John Gosden	283	95	33.57%	+£70.91
James Ferguson	22	7	31.82%	+£3.07
Saeed bin Suroor	147	44	29.93%	-£17.94
Charlie Appleby	191	57	29.84%	-£23.28
Sean Curran	21	6	28.57%	+£0.25

Top trainers by Strike Rate – handicaps

Name Of Trainer	Runners	Winners	Strike Rate	Profit/Loss to BSP
Kim Bailey	15	6	40.00%	+£42.29
Gavin Cromwell	15	6	40.00%	+£42.29
Charlie Appleby	96	35	36.46%	+£7.62
Saeed bin Suroor	103	37	35.92%	+£47.98
Simon and Ed Crisford	47	15	31.91%	+£36.97

Top trainers by Profit – non-handicaps

Name Of Trainer	Runners	Winners	Strike Rate	Profit/Loss to BSP
Tom Dascombe	319	58	18.18%	+£324.90
Marco Botti	390	65	16.67%	+£261.95
Declan Carroll	31	2	6.45%	+£171.91
Phil McEntee	87	5	5.75%	+£153.16
Richard Hannon Jnr	286	51	17.83%	+£129.00

Top trainers by Profit – handicaps

Name Of Trainer	Runners	Winners	Strike Rate	Profit/Loss to BSP
Micky	92	11	11.96%	+£187.50

Hammond				
Robert Stephens	85	10	11.76%	+£147.44
Bill Turner	86	11	12.79%	+£112.71
Christopher Kellett	68	3	4.41%	+£108.39
Andi Brown	32	8	25.00%	+£107.08

Top trainer/jockey combos by Strike Rate – non-handicaps

Name of Trainer/Jockey	Qualifiers	Winners	Strike Rate	Profit/Loss to BSP
John Gosden/William Buick	17	10	58.82%	+£14.03
John Butler/Adam Kirby	12	7	58.33%	+£11.95
George Baker/Pat Cosgrave	11	5	45.45%	+£6.45
Charlie Appleby/James Doyle	25	11	44.00%	+£4.99
William Haggas/Tom Marquand	31	13	41.94%	+£11.65

Top trainer/jockey combos by Strike Rate – handicaps

Name of Trainer/Jockey	Qualifiers	Winners	Strike Rate	Profit/Loss to BSP
Conrad Allen/Jimmy Quinn	10	5	50.00%	+£58.17
Charlie Appleby/Kevin Stott	11	5	45.45%	+£4.26
Tim Easterby/Andrew Mullen	10	4	40.00%	+£24.31
Chris Dwyer/Raul Da Silva	15	6	40.00%	+£9.43
David	13	5	38.46%	+£28.85

Simcock/Martin Harley				

Top trainer/jockey combos by Profit – non-handicaps

Name of Trainer/Jockey	Qualifiers	Winners	Strike Rate	Profit/Loss to BSP
Marco Botti/Stefano Cherchi	26	2	7.69%	+£140.66
Richard Fahey/David Nolan	30	4	13.33%	+£100.03
Michael Bell/Hayley Turner	26	6	23.08%	+£98.65
Karl Burke/Ben Curtis	17	4	23.53%	+£59.54
David Loughnane/Ben Curtis	11	2	18.18%	+£56.79

Top trainer/jockey combos by Profit – handicaps

Name of Trainer/Jockey	Qualifiers	Winners	Strike Rate	Profit/Loss to BSP
Micky Hammond/Aiden Brookes	17	3	17.65%	+£125.89
Tony Caroll/Mollie Phillips	65	7	10.77%	+£122.33
David Evans/Gina Mangan	41	6	14.63%	+£91.25
John Ryan/Jack Mitchell	13	2	15.38%	+£83.08
Mandy Rowland/Rob Hornby	39	4	10.26%	+£78.35

Profit or Loss backing the unnamed favourite – non-handicaps

Runners	Winners	Strike Rate	Profit/Loss to BSP
5143	2002	38.93%	-£59.30

Profit or Loss backing the unnamed favourite – handicaps

Runners	Winners	Strike Rate	Profit/Loss to BSP
9735	2740	28.15%	-£1.20

Profit or loss backing the unnamed second favourite - non-handicaps

Runners	Winners	Strike Rate	Profit/Loss to BSP
4955	1069	21.57%	-£71.52

Profit or loss backing the unnamed second favourite - handicaps

Runners	Winners	Strike Rate	Profit/Loss to BSP
9108	1685	18.50%	-£23.22

Profit or Loss backing horses who won last time out - non-handicaps

Runners	Winners	Strike Rate	Profit/Loss to BSP
1600	381	23.81%	-£73.77

Profit or Loss backing horses who won last time out - handicaps

Runners	Winners	Strike Rate	Profit/Loss to BSP
9113	1740	19.09%	-£71.07

Profit or loss backing Top-Weights in handicaps

Runners	Winners	Strike Rate	Profit/Loss to BSP
11746	1755	14.94%	-£122.23

Most profitable sires – non- handicaps

Dandy Man	190	19	10.00%	+£633.07

Animal Kingdom	11	2	18.18%	+£293.22
Red Ransom	11	4	36.36%	+£252.77
Ad Valorem	13	1	7.69%	+£202.00
Olympic Glory	14	3	21.43%	+£176.89

Most profitable sires – handicaps

Avonbridge	292	38	13.01%	+£405.54
Hellvelyn	70	3	4.29%	+£382.54
Iffraaj	573	80	13.96%	+£244.95
Aqlaam	196	24	12.24%	+£198.29
Dandy Man	483	50	10.35%	+£176.31

Testimonials:

"Sean and I have worked together for many years now, and his knowledge of racing is well known and respected throughout the industry. If the articles and opinion shared with readers of News - The World of Sport are any indication as to just how valuable this book will be to punters, then it's a "must have" weapon in your punting arsenal. If you do not bet using stats, you will lose more often than you win and, whether you bet for profit or fun, you need this on your side"

Ron Robinson – Owner, The World of Sport

"Sean Trivass is better known as the 'Statman' to my readers and has contributed excellent comprehensive articles on horse racing for my monthly newsletter What really Wins Money. His stats angles are totally unique and a real deep dive into the world of horse racing stats based betting angles.

He's looked at jockeys, trainers, race courses, sires and dams (breeding), the draw, the all weather, favourites, 2nd and 3rd favourites , ground conditions, race distance, handicaps versus non-handicap and many other angles, for both the horse racing backer and layer.

There have been some real eye-catching finds from Sean's work, some of which I use myself. This guy knows his onions! "

Clive Keeling – What Really Wins Money

"Statistics can be presented in many a varied manner for varied reasons and we are right to retain a sceptical mind of them and how and why they are revealed. However, with horse racing they are a vital component and my colleague Sean Trivass is an equally vital component in collating and interpreting them for our use.

Watching, listening, reading Sean's dissection of a field using his calibrated statistics is a racing marvel. He professes to not liking full-sized handicap fields, but in reality he is in his element pouring over the variables using his statistics as he slices and dices the field into a logical order for the likes of you and I to understand.

Group 1 elite contests to the full field handicaps are all part of Sean's vision and depth of years of experience. From watching the world's best on the track to a humble maiden, he approaches each contest with the same enthusiasm to find the outcome

I have watched and enjoyed Sean's work for twenty years as we have travelled to race meetings in many parts of the globe and when back home in Australia he is my guide for UK racing. Racing is international, broadcasting 24 hours a day somewhere in the world, and Sean's delving into the statistics give us all a steady platform to participate".

Rob Burnet
Editor
Thoroughbrednews.com.au

Finally, should you have any questions (no abuse thank you, all of this has been written in good faith) or just want to know a little bit more about my upcoming projects and books, feel free to contact me via www.writesports.net

©Sean Trivass 2023

Printed in Great Britain
by Amazon